WHAT DID GOD SAY?

By

Alvin Deal

TABLE OF CONTENTS

INTRODUCTION

Why did I ask, "What did God say?" Matthew 4:4 says that Jesus said unto the enemy, "Man should not live on bread alone but by every word that proceeds out of the mouth of God."

I know what E.F. Hutton says. I know what my state legislature said. I know what the president has said. I know what historians said. I know what my doctor has said. I know what my mama and my daddy said, but there were times in my life that I did not know what God said. When I found out that God created everything, I needed to know what he said. Why? Because it's important; because He is the creator, and He is the one that put me into existence. What I'm saying is... I need to know what he said AND what is He saying. SO, I went on a journey to find out what God said about Alvin Deal, first.

What Did God Say?
Where do I start? I did not know anything about God. I would ride the school bus in the morning going to elementary and middle school and I used to talk to the Sun, and not knowing anything about God, but something inside of me said there was somebody; there's a higher power, a being somewhere. I did not know it at the time, but I was talking to Him then. My brother Lloyd told me there is no such thing as God and

that he was a made-up deity that people used to keep you in line.

Years later, when I had the experience of getting born again, I began to search the scriptures to find out if there is a God and once, I came into the knowledge that if I believe in my heart and confess with my mouth I can be saved. The bible said, "To whosoever will, let Him come," and I was one of those that came to him, just like I was not believing in Him, not knowing a whole lot about Him, but searching for Him.

And so, when I searched for him, I found him and after finding him, I still did not

know a whole lot about what He said. And I had to begin to go on this journey for more information. Is this really God, is this me or is this something that somebody wrote in a book. So, I had to dig and do a little research to answer the question, 'Is this truly God?' While on this journey I began to ask more questions…

"What did God say specifically about my health"?

"What did he say specifically about my relationship?"

"What is my purpose?"

"What is His plan for me?"

So, there were lots of questions in my mind even before I came to know Jesus as my personal Lord and Savior. I knew I needed Jesus in my life, but I had not learned anything about who He really was before I was born again. So, when someone gave me a bible, I began to study, day and night, looking for answers…especially now that they were saying I was a "new creature."

They say I am a new creature, but I still had the same thought patterns and was still doing some of the same things. I had to find out how I am to talk; how I am to treat my brothers and sisters; and am I different. And so, I began to read the book and the book began to give me direction.

I had an older brother who had gotten saved two months prior to me coming to the Lord. My mother was a member of a Baptist church, and my father was a member of an AME church, however, we did not go to church, except maybe on Christmas and those revival days where you go out and eat big meals. We were not church going people. When I returned from Orlando Florida, I found out my brother, Andrew, had gotten saved. He started "witnessing" to me and told me that I needed to go to church. I had just lost my girlfriend, lost my job, lost my car, and almost lost my mind. So, I was kind of distraught. Andrew noticed my distress and he told me to come to church. My mindset at the time was not thinking about the Lord but what I had heard about church. I heard that you could meet some nice girls over at the church, so I figured I could go and get myself a new girlfriend. That was my thought pattern at the time. Again, remember we grew up in a family who did not really attend church. My mother and father only went every now and then, and I remember going as a teenager every blue moon. So, when I got born again and came into the kingdom of God, I began to be viewed differently because now, instead of every blue moon, I was in church on Sunday morning, Sunday evening, Tuesday night for bible study, choir practice and men's fellowship on Saturday.

As time passed, I could see my family was slowly changing, because my older sister was now an active member in the Baptist church attending regularly with her husband and children. My other sisters started going to church on a regularly basis along with their family. My sisters were not living with us by my teenage years. So, my sibling's thought about me was just like it was before I moved to Florida, not sure of my intensions.

They were happy though about me being saved. They would say with enthusiasm and excitement...He got saved. He is doing good now. He is not drinking, he is not smoking,

and he is in church every Sunday now, so he is better than what he was, and we are glad about that. We do not have to bail him out of jail or peel him off the road after a car wreck... so yes, they were glad about my change. I know you want to know how all this began and what were the steps that I took to turn my life around. Well, if you keep reading this book, I will show you how I learned how to put into practice What God Has Said for your life and family. I promise you that if you will follow the example of the Word of God that I used you to will have a successful life. Let's get started!

MY JOURNEY TO FAITH

I graduated from high school in 1978. Being a promiscuous young man, my girlfriend and I became teen parents shortly after graduation. As a result, we moved from Greenwood, South Carolina to Orlando, Florida. We lived at 414 Cypress Street in Orlando with her grandparents in one of the rooms in the back of their home. I had a job offer at Disney World but turned it down because I did not want to shave my mustache. I was 18 years old, and naïve about things of the real world. So, I turned that job down and gained employment with Power Concrete on International Drive, creating door headers, window seals, lentils, and other concrete things of that nature. My expectation when I left Greenwood, South Carolina was to return successful, with plenty of money to show everyone that I was doing well and could afford to obtain anything in life that I wanted from fancy cars to luxurious homes.

I had a high school education, a girlfriend, a baby on the way, and a good mind, so when I moved to Orlando Florida, this big metropolis of a city, a melting pot and the vacation capital of the world, I thought I was properly prepared to get our life started, but instead of properly planning for a family and becoming a father, I was in this big city enjoying myself. To make matters worse I had become a compulsive gambler. I soon learned how difficult it was to quit this addiction. I would gamble away all my money. My addiction to gambling had become priority. Every week I would go to the bank, cash my paycheck, and squander my entire paycheck on alcohol and gambling. I would then go home empty handed and drunk.

Six months into this gambling addiction, I had an epiphany. I got up one morning heavily impressed with the thought and notion of going to church. So, on this Sunday morning, I got out of bed, got dressed and left home in search of the nearest church. I decided to look first in our neighborhood because I was clueless as to where any other churches were located. So, I drove around the neighborhood and stopped at a church on Washington Street in Orlando. It was an AME church. I entered the church and found a seat near the door. I came in during the middle of the announcement period. If I can recall the announcement, it was about an upcoming trip the church was preparing for. So, I sat there for about 15 minutes, I had heard enough about this trip, and I got up and walked out. Although I walked out, I could still feel that heavy feeling from earlier that morning. After arriving home, I sat in the car and listened to gospel music for about an hour or more. I did not know what this feeling was, but the short time in the church and the gospel music lifted me and I felt I was alright.

However, from that point on, my life began to go downhill. There was a situation that happened next that would turn my already upside-down world, upside down again. There was a young man who lived in the neighborhood, and he asked if I would give him a ride to the school because he was involved in the after-school program there and did not want to miss participating in helping the younger ones in our neighborhood. Well, at least this is the reason he gave me for needing a ride. I drove him to the school, and he asked me to wait for him, so I waited. He came back about 30 minutes later, and he had a piece of equipment with him. I asked him what it was, and he told me the teacher gave it to him and said he could have it. I thought nothing else of it, because his story sound reasonable and believable, so my response to his answer was simply, "Ok, no problem but where is my $6 for gas, you promised me for bringing you over here." He said he wanted to go ahead and sell the piece of equipment so he could give me my gas money. At this point, I drove him into downtown Orlando to a pawn shop. He again asked me to wait for him while he took the machine into the shop to pawn and get some money to pay me. So, as I wait, a police cruiser pulls up behind me about 15 minutes later and I see two officers get out of the police cruiser and walk up to my car. At the time I still had a South Carolina driver's license as well as a South Carolina tag on my car and I am thinking the officers were just seeing the out-of-town tags and were just checking for validation of the tags. So, one officer approached the car, and the other officer went into the pawn shop. He talked briefly with me and then asked, "What's your name?" I told him Alvin Deal. Then he asked what I was doing here? I told him I had brought a friend downtown to the pawn shop so he could pawn a piece of equipment and give me my gas money. I was just being honest with him. The officer gestured and said a simple "ok." Then he asked if I had any drugs on me or any drugs in the car. I said, "No sir, why did you ask me that?" The officer said, "We received a call about your friend in there from the pawn shop owner. He recognized a state ID or government ID on the equipment and the equipment had been stolen from the school." I said, "Sir, I had no idea. This is a young man in the neighborhood that had asked me to give him a ride to participate in the after-school program." Well, of course the officer did not believe I was telling him the truth and that night I got arrested. My car was impounded, and I stayed in jail for one night. I was released on my 'own recognizance' the next day. Prior to being released, I had to go on pre-trial intervention, and as I wait for my release all I could do was nervously pace back and forth. During the pre-trial intervention I was told that I had lost my car and was being charged with a felony. I was appointed a public defender and so I told him my story and I find out later that the young man was a juvenile.

ON TRIAL

Even though the young man was a juvenile this guy had a full beard at 17. Because of his features I never suspected he was still under the age of 18. And here I am 18 (almost 19) years old, and they are going to charge me with a felony. During a meeting with the public defender, he told me of a conflict we had. It turned out the same public defender was also appointed to help the other young man. After realizing this he said to me, "I'm his attorney also I can't represent you now." I was assigned another attorney, who, after receiving my information, was able to get the other guy to say that I did not have any knowledge of what he had planned or had done. Unfortunately, by this time the State had taken up the case and wanted to prosecute anyway. Because of this I had to continue through the channels of the judicial system. I opted for a plea deal where they dropped the charge from a felony to a misdemeanor and I was placed on 6 months' probation. After the 6 months expired, my record would be expunged. Now if that ordeal wasn't terrible enough, however, what made my life even more grievous and unbearable was that my girlfriend and daughter moved away. This also meant I lost a place to lay my head at her grandparent's home. I was fortunate to get a room in a boarding house on South Palmore Street near Orange Blossom Trail in Orlando Florida. That is considered the red-light district and since I also lost my job during this trial, I had to go out into Orange Grove and pick oranges to make some money to survive. After living in this boarding room for about two months at that point, I had another epiphany, although I did not know it at the time it was God speaking to me. I heard a voice say to me, *"You need to go back home."* So, I worked in Orange Grove until I had enough money to buy a bus ticket. The night I was planning to go to the bus station to get my ticket for the next day, someone invited me to a card game. I started gambling because I still had this desire to want to come back home with money, you know looking good to impress my family and friends I ended up losing all that money. Fortunately, I had a nice somewhat expensive watch, and I sold that watch and thankfully got enough money for my bus ticket. My clothes were dirty, and I put them in a little raggedy suitcase, and I got on the bus headed back to Greenwood, South Carolina from Orlando Florida.

During the bus ride back to Greenwood, I was so hungry. But I did not have money for food. I did not have money for anything to drink and the lady that was sitting in the seat next to me was eating peanut butter crackers. She evidently gained a sense that I was hungry and offered me some of her crackers and I began to eat those crackers as though they were a full course meal. So here I am on this bus, returning to Greenwood and I did not have anything but my dirty clothes. I had lost my girlfriend, lost my car, and almost lost my mind. I lost everything including my dignity. I was ashamed. I did not tell anyone where I was staying. I did not let anybody know I was back in town. One Saturday evening while walking from my mom's house headed to my brother's house, which was not too far-apart.

When Andrew saw me, he said, "Al, you need to go to church with me tomorrow morning." I am thinking yep that is a good idea; but I was thinking it for all the wrong reasons. I rationalized, by going to Andrew's church, I would get another girlfriend, get me another job, another car and I will be back to normal.

So I go to this church, and it is a church like no other. I went to the first Sunday morning service with Andrew. I could hear them joyously clapping their hands as I entered the church. The baby grand piano was playing. The B3 Hammond organ was playing, everyone was singing to the top of their voices, and I am thinking 'this is strange'. I had never been in a church like this before during the short occasions that I had attended church. And so, walking into this church and seeing the service was explosive.

Then the pastor stands up to preach and his stature is about 6'6". He begins preaching the word of God and he then stretches out his long arm and he said, "You're smoking dope!" And it looked like he was pointing at me. And then he said, "You're in the nightclubs!" And every time he spoke it looked like he was pointing directly at me. And he said, "You're chasing women, you're gambling and your midnight rambling!" And he just kept saying that and as he is talking, I am getting angry and I'm looking over at my brother thinking, "I'm going to beat you up and I'm going to beat that preacher up!" Then I looked up at the preacher who was still six feet-six inches tall, and I thought, "Well maybe I will not beat the preacher up. Maybe I can get some nails to put under his tire and flatten the tires on his car; but I'm definitely going to beat my brother up because he told this preacher all my business and now everybody knows me. How can I get a girlfriend in the church when everybody knows he is talking about me in his preaching."

I never had a church experience like this before. Then after pointing at me through the sermon, he said, "God will forgive you of everything you have ever done. He will forgive every lie you have told." He said, "God will wipe the plate clean." Now when he made this statement about a clean plate, I knew about that because I come from a family of 16. There were 16 of us that lived in the same household. Ten boys and six girls and if you did not get to the dinner table in a timely fashion, you may have missed out on some of the better portions of the dinner and when you did get your plate, you wiped it clean. So, when the preacher said *"He'll wipe it clean"* I was looking at my life. I had a lot of blemishes in my life; a lot of things I have said and done wrong in my life, and he said, *"He'll wipe it clean."* And from that point on the wind left my jaws and the preacher said, "God will forgive you of everything you've ever done." And then he said, "The wage of sin is death, but the gift of God is eternal life." So, something had convicted me.

BECOMING A NEW CREATION

As I said, the visit to Andrew's church was eye-opening. What I saw and heard at this church I had never experienced before. My sister-in-law was sitting right in front of me, right next to her husband Andrew. I tapped her on the shoulder, and in a low voice I asked if she could take me up to the front of the church so that I can be saved. She turned around, looked at me and she said, "You have to get it yourself" and turned right back around. In the meantime, the preacher was still preaching and inviting lost souls to come to Jesus. "'Give your life to him." And so, I tapped her on the shoulder again because this thing and feeling was just stirring me. She turned around and I said, "Could you at least walk up there with me and help me get saved?" Once again, she said, "I told you, you have to get it yourself." Maybe six minutes into his alter call, 'something' stirs me to get up out of my chair. I got out of my chair and walked to the altar and next thing I knew I was down on my knees asking what must I do or what is next, not knowing exactly what to say because I was expecting what I've been told such as you'll see a light, you're going to fall out, you're going to roll on the floor, God's going to do it all. And none of that happened. After about five minutes, a brother kneeled beside me and he asked me, "Do you believe Jesus died on the cross?" I said "Yes." He asked, "Do you believe God raised him from the dead?" I said "Yes." He said, "If you believe that in your heart and profess it with your mouth you shall be saved. I said to him, "I thought we were supposed to get a feeling;" and he said, "The feeling will come later, some people feel it immediately and some people do not. And then he asked me if I believe that I am saved right now, and did I repent of my sins?" I said, "Yes I did." He then said the preacher was going to ask for a testimony at the end of the altar call. He told me to go back to my seat and if I believe that I was saved he wanted me to stand up and give a testimony. And so, I went back to my seat and of course the preacher did ask is there any testimonies, and I stood up and the preacher asked, "What has the Lord done for you? I said, "I believe He saved me today!" The entire church started clapping and the music began. Then the preacher instructed me to clap my hands. Remember that I did not feel anything when I was at the alter giving my life to Christ. Then, the preacher said, "Praise God! Clap your hands, praise God!" I tell you the sound of the preacher's voice and the people clapping made me lift my hands and clap. It was as if I was seeing my hands being freed from whatever was previously holding them down.

That was my experience of becoming Born again. The weight and distress from my experience in Florida was lifted from my shoulders. I had lost everything because I decided to help someone, so I thought, to being arrested and going through the pre-trial intervention, to losing my family and job, and then having to come back to Greenwood feeling defeated, was all lifted from my shoulders. That is how I came to the knowledge of Jesus Christ as my personal Lord and Savior.

BABY STEPS IN MY NEW LIFE

Well, when I first got saved and gave my life to Christ and came into the kingdom of God, I was taking those baby steps to turn my life around. During this same time, I still had some marijuana at home, and I had a six pack of beer at home. So, when I got home after being saved reality hit me. The questions in my head were, *"So, what are you going to do with your marijuana?"* And so immediately the enemy started talking to me and saying, "You know God created everything, and you know how he created the herbs, and herbs is what the Native Americans smoked in the peace pipe. And, God said he created everything, and it was good, so do you think the Bible lied." The enemy continued talking to me all the way home. So, when I arrived, I lit up a joint and I smoked it. Then, I called my old girlfriend to tell her the good news. I had previously been in communication with her, and she had planned to come to visit. When I called her, I said, "Listen I got saved" and then immediately asked if she was coming. Her response was not what I wanted to hear because she said she was not coming over. I remember, suddenly, I began to get angry, and I began to curse and swear at her over the phone. My mother was in the room, and she said, "I thought you said you got saved." Immediately there was a conviction within me.

So, I hung the phone up, took the marijuana that was in my pocket and flushed it down the commode. I took the beer and poured it out and did not drink any more. I repented to the Lord and promised that I would not do it again. The only thing I did not give up at that time was my cigarettes because cigarettes was the hardest thing to give up. Also, the lust that I had for women was hard to overcome, because when I got around good-looking women I would sweat at the forehead. I had to have them. I was inundated with lust. So those things I had to work on...cigarettes and lust for women.

First, I started working on the cigarettes, quickly realizing I was trying to stop on my own, and of course, I could not. I had to ask God for help. I had to have one after meals, when I was in the bathroom and while having a conversation with someone. So, I prayed and asked the Lord to please help with the habit of smoking cigarettes. I knew it was not good for the body. Even the Surgeon General gave us the warning of the products/smoking could cause cancer. I remember thinking, Lord, I need some help and I was also instructed by the pastor to fast. So, I fasted for 3 days. I abstained from food, and I did drink water. On the third day of my fast, my girlfriend came for a visit. I picked her up from the bus station and she was still a smoker.

We were riding down the road and she lit up a cigarette, so I grabbed her pack of cigarettes and took out a cigarette and lit it. As I took that first pull suddenly, it was as if something or someone hit me in the chest and hit my mouth. I heard this voice say, *"I thought you asked me to take the taste out of your mouth?"* and I threw that cigarette out the window, grabbed the pack of cigarettes and threw the pack out of the window. She screamed, "Why did you do that...you know those are my cigarettes!" We did not go back and get them, but I had to give her money to buy another pack. But throwing the cigarettes out, all I could think of was that I did it...and that was one of the steps towards ending the craving. I had gotten a victory over those cigarettes.

My other vices such as the anger, the rage, and the lust, I had to dive into the word of God. In Ephesians 5:26, He says, "...by the washing of the water of the word." I had to keep putting that word in front of me, speaking that word and this is exactly what I did. I stayed in church. Sunday morning, Sunday evening, Tuesday night bible study, Thursday, and Friday night for 'Joy' Night service and then Saturday we would work around the church. So, I began to occupy myself with being in church and that would fulfill a lot of my times.

TEMPTATIONS

After being saved, I started hanging around some of my friends again, and they turned their noses up at me. These were the friends I used to drink and smoke marijuana with. While hanging out with them one day, one of my closest friends, rolled up a joint and blew it in my face. He said, "Come on, I know you're going to smoke; you know you like this...I know how you like this." He would also offer me beer and they would taunt and tease me on a regular basis, but I stayed with the Word. I stayed with it, but it was a struggle being caught in the middle of my new life choices and my friends. I made this commitment to the Lord, and I decided to plan to stay around this church and be around church people.

My brother Johnny felt I would stick around for only a couple of weeks. He knew how I was and felt I was not going to last long because I liked the club life, and I liked to drink. He would say, "You like to smoke, and you like the women. You are not going to last long." And so, I stayed around the church. For some strange reason I shipped all the church services.

I stayed away from the church for a week. I did not go to one of the services and one of the members visited me at my home, out in the country, and encouraged me. This was encouraging to me. Then another church member came out. Not only did they visit me but invited me out to lunch. I was so empowered and so encouraged by the visits because that helped me to get my spiritual footing. I knew that somebody cared. I knew that God was reaching out to help me, even in those difficult times, where I was struggling...with my habits of cigarettes and with lust. I was struggling with my old friends. Even though I come from a large family God gave me a whole new set of brothers and sisters in Christ. Some of my family members withdrew from me now that I am different and have changed my behavior. I am talking really different from what they were used to. I am going to different places. I am hanging around different people. So, those that did not like my new lifestyle kind of withdrew from me; but they never stop loving me. They loved me from a distance because I had changed my way of walking. I changed the things that I was doing and the people I was spending my time with. So, in the end, staying in the word and staying in church caused me to find a secure place where I could continue to grow.

WHY DOES GOD SPEAK TO US?

I did not understand that God speaks all the time. Prior to my transformation I did not understand the voice of God and I did not know what was going to happen after I gave my life to Christ. It sounded like trial and error. As the years pass, I learned that God speaks to us about different subjects; God speaks on different topics, and he is always giving us information. He put information in 66 books, with so many different authors, so that we can understand what he is wanting to teach us. Once we come to an understanding of what

God said about the various topics of life, we see that God has answered every question, and he has given a solution for every problem. All we must do is find out what God says and be willing to allow God to teach us what we need to know.

Jesus gives us an introduction into what God says when he confronted the enemy out in the wilderness. In the gospel according to St. Matthew, the Fourth chapter, the bible said that Jesus, after being baptized by John, was led into the wilderness where he fasted for 40 days and 40 nights. And afterwards he was hungry and, in that 3rd, verse, it says that Satan came to him and tempted him and said, "If you be the son of God will you turn these stones into bread". And Jesus answered, in that fourth verse, "It is written that man shall not live by bread alone, but by every word that proceeded out of the mouth of God." Hence, we see that Jesus is telling Satan that man does not live by natural things alone, but by every word that comes from the mouth of God. So, it is in our best interest to begin to find out what God Says.

I needed to begin to find out what God was saying to me. Once I began to find out what God says, then I began to make those words applicable to my life. So that put me on the journey to find out what God was saying about Alvin Deal? What did God say about finance? What did God say about healing? What did God say about money? What did God say about children and love? What did God say about the kingdom? I had to really build a trust in what God says. Remember, at that point, I was an early believer trying to figure out what God was saying to me. So, I looked in the scripture. I went to Psalms 119, verse 89 which said, "Forever oh Lord is that word settled the heavens." Then I went to Titus 1:2 where it said that God cannot lie, then I went to Hebrews 6:18 where it says, "...by two immutable things, in which it was impossible for God to lie..." I went back into the Old Testament in Numbers 23:19 where it says that "God is not a man that he should lie; neither the son of man that he should repent..." He said it, He will do it, and He will bring it to pass. Then I read Proverbs 3:5-6 where it says, "Trust in the Lord with all thine heart; and lean not unto thine own understanding. In all thy ways acknowledge him and he shall direct thy path." So, I was trying to find out, is this God trustworthy? And all these scriptures were backing up the fact that he stands behind His word. In Isaiah 55:11 he says, "So shall my word be that goeth forth out of my mouth: it shall not return void, but it shall accomplish that which I please and it shall prosper in the thing whereto I sent it." After reading that I said, 'oh my God.' I began to find out that he is a trustworthy God. I found other scriptures in the New Testament such as Matthew 24:35 that says, "Heaven and earth will pass away but my words shall not pass away." So, I begin to find out truly, what did God say? And then I read in Romans 3:4, "Let God be true and let every man be a liar." And once I found that out, I began to say I need to find out, what is God saying now? So, I went to Hebrews again, the First chapter, and it says that God had spoken in sundry times and different divers' places and spoke through his prophets. And so, I began to go on this journey to find out what God said. What is God saying? And once I found out God is a trustworthy God and that his word faileth not, and then I began to stumble upon other scriptures like Jeremiah 1:12 which says that he hastens to perform his word. Once I began to conclude that I can trust God and that God's word will not return void, I began to dig into the word of God even deeper.

I began to find out what God said about Alvin Deal. Who am I in Christ Jesus. I read in St. John 1:12, where it says, "To them that believeth in him or received him, to them gave He power to become the sons of God...." So, God says that I, Alvin, am a son of God and not only am I a son of God, but I read another scripture that said I am an heir of God and a joint heir with Christ Jesus. So, I began to go to these other scriptures, and I found out in Romans 8:31 that he said since God is for me, he is more than the whole world against me. I found out in 1st John 4:4 where he said "...greater is he that is in me than he that is in the world." Then I went back to Romans 8:37 where he said in all these things, I am more than a conqueror. The more I read these scriptures, I began to build up my self-esteem and confidence in God, especially upon discovering that God could not lie, and that I can do all things through

Christ who strengthens me as it tells me in Philippians 4:13.

Then I read about John the Baptist who was heard preaching the gospel in the wilderness near the river Jordan while baptizing people; and whole cities were coming out to be baptized by him, even church people were coming. The Pharisees, the Sadducees, the Herodians, and the Scribes were coming because they saw the great crowds. So, they asked John if he was the one who was prophesied. They asked him who was he and who gave him the authority to do this? Take notice John's response in St. John 1:23. John said, "I am the voice of one crying in the wilderness. Make straight the way of the Lord...." In verse 27 John also told them that he was not the One. That he (Christ) was coming after him and that he was not worthy to even bow down to untie Christ's shoelaces. I thought John's answer was so appropriate. I thought it was unique because he did not say I am Zachariah's son; my daddy works up there in the temple. He did not say, I am Elizabeth's son, y'all know my mother was old when she had me. He did not say any of that. He said exactly what was said about him in the scripture in Isaiah; a voice of one crying in the wilderness. John repeated exactly what God said about him, the true report of what God said about him. And so, when I begin to say what God says about me, I began to fulfill the scripture of Amos 3:3 where it asked the question how can two walk together except, they agree. So now God and I agree, and that place of agreement is powerful.

From that stance I began to build myself up in the word of God. Colossians 3:16 says, "Let the word of Christ dwell in you richly...." I begin to allow God's word to dwell in me richly. I began to sing hymns and spiritual songs making a melody in my heart to the Lord. Why... because now I was saying what God says about me.

I am reminded of the story of Gideon. His people were under attack and Gideon was hiding and God came to Gideon in the voice and said "Gideon, you mighty man of valor." Now look at the position of Gideon. He is hiding, he is fearful, he's afraid, he's timid, he's shy and he's angry because now God is calling him; however, God is not calling him afraid, timid, or fearful. God said you are a mighty man of valor. God did not call him based on how he felt, God called him based on how God saw him. God sees us victorious. God sees us healed. God sees us whole. God sees us healthy and based on that premise, I began to say, this is how God sees me. When I began to see myself the way God saw me, I began to speak in agreement with the way God sees me. When I discipline myself to speak as God sees me, it builds my esteem, it causes me to transform my thinking and it brings me to a place whereby I begin to see myself differently than what is being portrayed in the mirror. I began to see myself by the mirror of God's word instead of the mirror atop the dresser in my bedroom.

I AM THE LORD THAT HEALETH THEE

As I stayed on that journey of speaking God's word, saying what God's word says, I found myself in a trial. In 1990 I was diagnosed with cancer. At this point in my life, I now had this Revelation of saying what God's word said, and now I found myself confronted with a natural circumstance, with a physical condition in my body. It started off with a lump in on the side of my neck. I was not feeling any discomfort at all, but it looked like a bee had stung me on the side of my neck. It had not gone down after three or four days and one of my family members suggested I go to the doctor to get the lump examined. I contacted a friend who was early in his position of practicing medicine and went to see him. He began to examine the lump. Because he was still an intern during this time, he wanted to refer me to someone else who was a friend of his in the medical field, someone who understood Internal medicine. As this doctor examined me, he said he needed to move forward with performing a biopsy. In fact, he wanted to do it that same day. In my mind I am thinking they are going to stick a little needle in my neck, pull out a little piece, and that is it. They sedated me and when I woke up, I had an inch and a half cut on my neck where they had pulled out one of my lymph nodes. The doctors told me they think it could be cancerous and they needed to send the tissue to the lab to be sure. Once the results were in, they would send them to me. So, two days later, I received a phone call, and they told me it is cancerous. So now I am faced with how to respond after hearing the results... I must either say what God says or say what the doctors have said. I have got to decide to agree with God's word, so I had to find out what God said about my healing and what God said about my health. So, when I got the phone call that it was malignant, of course at that moment I decided and I said, "By his stripes I am healed!" I began to speak First Peter 2:24, "Jesus himself bore my sins in his own body on a tree," so that me Alvin Deal, "being dead to sin would live unto righteousness: by his stripes, I was healed."

Now I began to dig into the word of God to find out what God said about my healing. Of course, my natural man is still strong. He is still up here, he still sees what he sees, he is still feeling what he feels, and he still sees the doctor report. Remember, the doctor has been to educational institutions for eight and sometimes twelve years to gain an education about biology, the physical anatomy and how it works; so yes, he is smarter than I am, and he knows more than I know. And of course, I was looking to him for an answer.

For the first three weeks of this ordeal, I confessed the words I am healed but I had a real physical thing that I needed to deal with. I saw this cancer and I got this information, and, in my mind, I had not been quite renewed to the point where I just settled in on what

God said because I was new on this journey still trying to find out what God said about healing. I continued with doctor appointments and follow up testing and on the third test, the doctors told me they will need to dig into my bone marrow; they needed to drill into my hip bone. The doctor told me what they were going to do and that it should be maybe a 15–20-minute procedure. Next, I found myself laying on my stomach and they are getting ready to drill into my hip bone on each side. The doctor has an intern with him and numbed the area and they gave me a little wooden stick to put in my mouth and asked me to bite down on the small stick. They begin to drill and 15, 20, 35, 40 minutes go by, and they are still not in. I am grunting and soon the procedure became painful because the Novocain or whatever they gave me was not working that well. After about an hour, I finally said quietly, "Lord let them in" and suddenly, poof, they were in. So, now they had to dig in on the other side, so I prayed before they got started on the other side and it took about 20 minutes, and they were able to get into the bone. I was 30 years old and had never been sick a day in my life, except for "normal stuff" such as slight cold or headache here and there. I was healthy, playing basketball and doing all those things, so I had strong bones and tissue.

After that procedure they called me to the doctor's office again. Throughout this ordeal, I am going through the process, and following the doctor's orders and was told now they need to take out my spleen. This was only a week after drilling into my bones which was very painful. Something on the inside of me was nagging and looking back, in hindsight, I know it was the Spirit of God. I remember asking the doctor, "What is the spleen? He said, the spleen is your blood filter and then he said, "You can live without it." I asked him, "What does the blood filter do?" And he said, "It filters your blood and if there are any cancerous cells in your blood stream then we can determine what stage the cancer is in your body." I then said to the doctor, Dr. Ramseur, "Listen, I am not going to do that; I'm going home, and I'll call you back and let you know whether I'll do that or not. I need to go home and settle myself." Dr. Ramseur then said, "You're not going to do it?" I said, "No, I'm going home." I then said to him, "I am a believer. I am going to believe and trust God." He replied, "A lot of people have trusted God and they have died." He then said, "You are going to die if you do not allow us to do this; not following through with this could kill you. I said to the doctor, "I shall not die but live and declare the work of the Lord. I did not know that was a scripture but later I found out that scripture was Psalms 118:17. I left his office. The reason he told me that I was going to die was based on his prognosis of what was happening in my body. I was having night sweats because of the cancer and all those other things that possibly would happen to me. Therefore, I did not fault him for saying what he said based on his education and his knowledge, along with what he had seen in the past, it was logical for him to make that type of prognosis from the natural standpoint. Since he was making his prognosis from the natural standpoint, I made my declaration in my spirit from God's standpoint...I shall not die but live and declare the work of the Lord. And so, I left his office and did not go back for what he wanted me to come back for.

Of course, I could not just stay away from the doctor, and do nothing. As I said earlier, I was on this journey to find out what God said about my healing. I had already found and began to speak 1Peter 2:24, then I went to Exodus 23:25 and saw, "So shall I serve the Lord and he'll bless my bread and bless my water; take sickness away from the midst of me." And the 26th verse says, "And I shall fulfil the number of my days in excellent fantastic exuberant health." I added the last part and then I turned to Exodus 15:26 where God said he will not allow any of the diseases that came upon the Egyptians to come upon me if I keep his commandments. The b section of the verse said, "...I am the Lord thy God that healeth thee." Then I turned to Isaiah 53:5 which states, "...he was wounded for my transgression, he was bruised for my iniquities and the chastisement for my peace was upon Him and with His stripes we are healed." So, I began to get these scriptures and began to confess these scriptures every day. As I got hold of the understanding of Psalms 107:20 which says, "He sent his word and healed me and delivered me from all my destruction." I found

Jeremiah 30:17, which says, "He restoreth health unto me and healed all my wounds..." I confessed those scriptures every day. During this entire time, I was still going to work, I was not going to the doctor anymore and I was not following his instructions, but I was constantly in the Word of God. I got up every morning before going to work and I started getting in the habit of walking down the dirt road near my home by myself and I took those scriptures and began to speak them out of my mouth, over and over as Romans 10:8 says, "...the word is nigh thee, even in thy mouth and in thy heart..." As I spoke them out of my mouth, those words got into my heart; they got into my mind and faith began to be released where the will of God is known. I found out that that is what God said about my healing. I had to share what I was doing when it came to declaring the word of God because other issues began to happen with me. Evidently, they left something inside of my neck. They didn't get all the nodes and during that year's period of time, the nodule began to grow, and my neck begin to bulge out bigger than what it was before. Throughout it all I am still confessing the Word of God. I was saying Isaiah 53:5, I was saying Jeremiah 30:17, I was saying Psalms 107:20, I was saying Exodus 23:25 and then I got a hold of Psalms 103:1 - 5 that says, "Bless the Lord O' my soul...; and forget not all his benefits...; who forgiveth all my iniquity...; ...healeth all my diseases; who satisfies my mouth with good things...; ...and crowning me with tender mercies and loving kindness." Hallelujah! Oh my God. I began to see that "He is satisfying my mouth" with good things. I had to keep these good things, which was the word of God, in my mouth at all times. The end of verse 5 says, "...He renewed my youth as the eagle".

I begin to stay with the word and confess that word daily on my way to work. I was confessing what God's word says with this knot on my neck. I was just confessing the word and still speaking it on my way back home. I limited my time in front of the television because I needed to focus on the word. Proverbs 4:20-21, 23 says, "My son, attend to my word; incline thine ears to my sayings. Let them not depart from thine eyes, keep them in the midst of thine heart. Keep thy heart with all diligence; for out of it are the issue of life." So, I had to keep my heart consecrated, keep it dedicated and focused on me declaring the Word. Remember the doctor told me I was going to die but God's word tells me I shall not die but live and declare the work of the Lord. Three months went by since I have seen the doctor, and I'm confessing the word continuously.

I purchased two acres of land because I was preparing to live, not preparing to die. I cleared the land, bought me a home, and had it put on the land during the midst of this health crisis. This whole time the knot on the side of my neck was swelling, it was getting bigger and eventually grew to 14 centimeters. I had pictures taken when it grew to that size. So, I still moved forward with getting my home ready for moving in. My mom began to contact me. She would see me often because I lived near her. She began to talk to me. She told me to make her a promise that once I got the land and the house and everything situated, that I would go back to the doctor. I did that in the first three months, and I told her sure I would go just to ease her mind and so now 6 months into confessing the word and no doctor visits.... and I am still going. I am feeling great. There is no pain in my body, only this big knot on my neck. People around me know that I had been diagnosed with cancer. And when one of my cousins died, from what I do not know. I was asked to do a prayer at his funeral. Now, I am a man of God, I'm a preacher and I'm in the pulpit during the funeral and about 300 people were there at the church. So, the people were looking at the casket, and they would look up at me. They would look down at the casket, and, then look back up at me. In my mind they are saying, 'casket means death and you're going to die!' So that scripture in Psalms 118:17 came back to my mind, I shall not die. I could not scream it out loud in the church, but I had to mutter it under my breath. Thinking back, I realize what was happening. I was being bombarded with thoughts of death from the congregation. They did not know what they were doing, but Satan knew what they were doing, and he was playing with my mind. So, I had to rely on the question, 'what did God say about my health?'

During the entire ordeal, I am meditating on God's word, I'm confessing the Lord's word daily, day in and day out. So, nine months go by, and this huge knot is still on my neck. Currently, I am still a pastor. I am pastoring a local Baptist Church in another county and so I had a revival one week and during one of the services I am laying hands on people during the revival. I am laying hands on people to be healed. There was a testimony of a lady whose mother had breast cancer. I laid hands on her. The lady called me three days later because her mother went back to the doctor and was told they could no longer find the cancer. I laid hands on a young girl during this revival who had all kinds of scabs in her head. A week later she was totally healed and in my private time I'm saying God I'm laying hands on people, and they are getting healed, what about me? I had questions. I am not in any way questioning the validity of God because it is already established that He cannot lie and that His word is already settled in the heavens. It was already established that heaven and earth will pass away before his word shall fail. However, my mind...I had to secure my mind on what God says. So, I left the questioning alone and kept confessing the word of God. In Hebrews 10:35 it states, "Cast not away your confidence, which hath great recompense of reward." So, I begin to get deep into that word again and just begin to confess that word. I found Psalms 19:14 where he said let the words of your mouth and the meditation of your heart be acceptable in thy sight oh Lord my strength, and my Redeemer." I begin to apply Psalms 119:105, which says to let God's word be a lamp unto my feet and a light unto my path, because I'm walking in this word and allowing God's word to be a lamp, letting God's word be a light. I began to search for Psalms 119:11. I had to let the word of God dwell in my heart. I had to "hide that word in my heart that I will not sin against you" ... saying it with my mouth and not saying anything other than what God said about it. I found another scripture, Mark 11:23, which says, "...whosoever shall say unto this mountain, be thou removed, (be thou plucked up) ...and shall not doubt in his heart but shall believe that those things which he saith shall come to pass; he shall have whatsoever he saith." I noticed in this scripture that the word 'saith' is mentioned three times. So, I said I am going to continue to say what God says because I will have what I say. So, I began to say, "By the stripes of Jesus I am healed." Remember now, I am already confessing the word, but now I'm getting more confident in it and this huge knot is still on my neck 11 months into me seeking and speaking what God says. The knot was not going down, but I am still going on about my business. I am not paying attention to it. I am not even looking at it. The only time I see it is when I am in the mirror. When I would look at, it thoughts would come to me saying "yes, the cancer is still there," and I have to cast down those thoughts as it says in 2Corinthians 10:3-5, "...though we walk in the flesh, we do not war after the flesh: For the weapons of our warfare are not carnal, but mighty through God to the pulling down of strong holds. Casting down imaginations, and every high thing that exalted itself against the knowledge of God and bringing into captivity every thought to the obedience of Christ." So, I had to bring those thoughts into captivity. In the midst of everything I was going through, my wife and I went through a separation. So, I am dealing with that in addition to my health. In Proverbs 23:7 it says as a man thinketh, so is he, so I could not allow those thoughts to get out of line with God's word. And, I had to deal with my physical nature; I had to deal with what people were saying and I had to deal with my emotions. So, once I brought them all under subjection, I was good. I was still going strong and doing well yet I have this 14-cm growth on the side of my neck still now 12 months into this. An entire year. Meanwhile, I got the house, I got the land, and I am doing good.

However, my mom came to me one day and she said, "You promised that you'll go back to the doctor... you promised, you promise me." And the Bible says that I am supposed to be like God; Ephesians 5:1 says, "be imitators, be followers of God as dear children and God never lied." So, I promised my mom that I was going to go back to the doctor. That was the last place I wanted to go because I was believing in God. I am standing on the promises of God. I am confessing what God's word says. I do not have any pain in my body, I'm feeling good but the only thing I got is this big 14-centimeter lump on the outside of my neck and I promised my mom something, so I'm in between a rock and a hard place. I asked myself the question, do I stand with God's word, or do I keep my promise? So, I had to find out what God said. And God said swear to your own hurt but do what is right. So, with that, I knew I had made her a promise and I did not want to be a liar, so I went to the doctor just to fulfill what my mom asked of me. When I went back to the doctor after 12 months the doctor was surprised to see me, and he simply ask, "What do you want?" in the nicest way possible, and I said "Well, doctor what do you have, what options do I have?", and he said, "I have got radiation and chemo. Which one do you want?" I thought the chemo was the strongest, so I told him to give me the chemo. He had me sign an agreement which I was not aware that's what it was at that time. I asked him why I had to sign an agreement because I had insurance and everything I needed. He told me that you walked out of my office the last time and if you walk out this time, your insurance will not pay anything. Based on that, I went ahead and signed it. Then he gave me two sheets of paper about the side effects and the things that could happen because of the chemotherapy. Then he told me I would have to do 8 months of this treatment and I did not like that, but I signed the agreement. He explained to me what was going to happen, and that I had to have treatment every two weeks. I cursed (not profanity but casting down) those things because I had found out in scripture that I have what I say, and I took those two sheets of paper and I said, "None of these things will happen to me- none of these things" and every day for the next three months I would go to the doctor's office every two weeks and have the treatment. I would come in on my lunch break and they would put the mustard seed, which is the chemotherapy, in my left hand.

Now here is the clincher, I did the first treatment for about an hour and a half, then went back to work. I did not get nauseous, or sick or throw up and I came back the next two weeks and I received the same procedure and still didn't get sick. Again, I went on my lunch break and went back to work. Somewhere between the second and the third treatment during the night the 14-centimeter growth on my neck was gone. I had about a week to go before my next appointment, and I could not wait to go to the doctor and tell him that I don't need to come back anymore. So, the appointment came, and I showed up early. I was so excited and so happy that this lump was gone after the whole year of having this thing on my neck and now it is not there... it just left out overnight. So, I went into the office, and I got in front of the doctor and I said, "Look, it's finally gone, I'm free, I'm healed!" The doctor didn't smile or show any excitement he just went to his desk, and he pulled out the agreement that I had signed and said, "Remember I told you you're not going to leave this time. You are going to finish these treatments." I remember I was about to get angry and walk out but I was so excited I decided it is not going to hurt anything so let me just finish this treatment. So, I said a simple okay, and I took the treatment that day. After two or three more treatments I started throwing up. Until then, I was getting regular treatments and still going back to work afterwards, but when I took the seventh or eighth treatments, I ended up in the hospital. I stayed in the hospital for two or three days. Everything shut down in my body and one of my pastoral friends came in and we prayed together. When I came out of the hospital, I remember asking the Lord what is going on and to please help me. He did not say anything to me, but he had spoken through the pastor and the pastor said to me, "You're already healed." I took that to say God had told me that I was healed, but because I had made a promise to my mom I went and did what I needed to do. So, I continued with the treatments and finished them. It had now been eight months of treatment. After the last treatment I went back to the doctor's office and he said, "Well, I see you finished that treatment, now we got another 6 weeks of radiation." I did not say anything, but I wanted to cry very loud and tell him no I was not, but I didn't say anything. He said he wanted me to show up at the hospital that following Monday for the radiation treatment. I just nicely nodded my head and left out of his office. I never reported to the hospital for the radiation treatment and that's been twenty-nine and a half years ago, and I've been healed from that cancer ever since. I have not even looked back. So, what did God say about healing... he said in Psalms 107 verse 20 that he sent his word, healed me, and delivered me from all my destruction. He said in 1st Peter 2:24, "Jesus himself bore my sins with his own body on the tree, that we, being dead to sin, should live unto righteousness by his stripes, I was healed." In Mark 11:23, he said I have what I say. So, I had to say what God said and come into agreement with what God said regardless of what I saw, regardless of what I felt, regardless of what the people were telling me. I had to stay with what God's word said. The scripture in Hebrews 10:23 told me that God is faithful, and I am to hold fast to my profession of faith without wavering because God is faithful who promised, and since God is a promise keeper, I got my healing.

I saw that I had gotten that victory and since I had that victory, it told me that the same process that it took to get my healing is the same process to get what God has for me concerning finances. I had to learn that, for my finances, God will be faithful, through the same process that he used for my other issues. I had to learn that God's word is true, God's word faileth not, and God's word will do exactly what it says. So, I continued this journey, now, to find out what God said about my finances.

I AM THE LORD GOD YOUR PROVIDER

During this time, I was a pastor, making only about $150 a week from the love offering at the church. I had a job, but my bills outweighed everything, so we were just trying to make ends meet. I began to get into the word of God again and find out what God said about my finances. Remember, I found out what He said about my healings, I did what He said, and I have not had a headache in 26 years. I have not had a cold in over 24 years. I am telling you once I found out what God's word says about healing, I have continued to confess these Scriptures daily. It is my daily regimen because I became disciplined concerning what God says about my healing, and I begin to step into divine health. Am I saying that I had not had an opportunity for a headache, opportunities for a cold, opportunities for those symptoms. Remember what it says in Ephesians 6:16, "Above all, taking the shield of faith...to quench all the fiery dots of the wicked," so what I did was stay with the word of God. The bible lets us know what Jesus said to the Jews that believed in him in St. John 8:31where it states, "...if you continue in my word then you will be my disciples indeed." The root word of discipline is disciple. In other words, the word disciple comes from the word discipline. If you have discipline regardless of what you feel, regardless of what is going on in your mind, regardless of what is going on around you, if you have the discipline to say what God said and stay with it. Discipline is enforced obedience.

And it says in Hebrews 11:6, "...he is a rewarder of them that diligently seek him." Jesus said to the Jews who believed in him, that if they continued in his word, they would be his disciples indeed (John 8:31). I am saying to you, if you continue confessing God's word, believing in God's word, and acting upon God's word concerning your healing, the healing will manifest itself. I remember the occasion that Jesus spoke to the fig tree in the eleventh chapter of the book of Mark. It tells us that he spoke to a fig tree because the fig tree was not in season, but the fig tree did not know that Jesus was the one that created it. Jesus is not limited by season. So, when Jesus spoke to the fig tree, the bible says he answered the fig tree. So, obviously the tree said Jesus, we don't have anything at this time," and Jesus said never again will men eat from you. When he spoke to the tree, the disciples heard him. However, when Peter and the rest of the disciples walked by the tree, the first time, they thought nothing happened. But a day later, Jesus walked right past the tree, and it was dried up from the roots. Jesus already knew what was going to happen. He already knew the validity of the word of God. The disciples, including Peter, were surprised. I will share with anyone, if you continue to trust in what God's word says, you too can speak to things. I spoke to that cancer, I spoke to my head, I spoke to my body and continue to speak to it because Proverbs 4:20 says to attend to the word; give it your attention and focus in on it, not just when you have calamity or when there is a sickness or disease but speak that word on a daily basis. Jesus said in John 8:31 to the Jews that believed in him, if they continued in my word, they will be my disciple indeed. And in the 32nd verse it says you will know the truth and the truth will make you free. And I say when you know the truth about healing God's way and the truth that you know that you become intimate with the word, like Adam knew Eve, (to become one intimately) it will manifest healing in your body.

So, I continue to confess God's word on a daily basis. I continue to live in this word and allowed it to become a lamp under my feet and a light on my path. I hid it in my heart so that I would not sin against Him. Because He is my strength and my redeemer, I let the words of my mouth and the meditations in my heart be acceptable in His sight (Psalm 19:14). I speak Psalms 119:89, that tells me God's word is forever settled in heaven, and God's word is forever settled in me. I will not be tossed to and fro because if I am tossed to and fro it means God is tossed to and fro. So, I am going to be exactly what God's word says I am. God's word says I'm healed, so I say I'm healed, even though I have pain that may come, and even though I have challenges, but I'm going to believe what God's word says. Mark 9:23 says that all things are possible for anyone that believes in Him. Without fail, I walk on this scripture daily, and I let the words of my mouth and the meditation of my heart be accepting in His sight. For the healing words that I speak to heal they have to be what God has already said about me. He said healing words in Isaiah 53:5 and I was healed in the word- he speaks healing in 1Peter 2:24 and I were healed. You got Isaiah looking forward, Peter looking backwards, and I am right in the middle of it. I can see back and look forward that I am healed from my past, I'm healed in my future, and I'm walking in Divine health in my present. That is the way I receive that word. That is how I know what God's word says. I understand that God is not a man that he should lie, nor the son of man that he should repent (Numbers 23:19). If He said it, He would do it. If he spoke it, it would come to pass. So, when I speak God's word concerning healing, just as it says in Psalms 103:20 that the Angels hearken unto the voice of his word, I also give God's word voice in the earth realm; and when I begin to say what God's word says it makes God's word legal in the earth realm; and when God's word is legal in the earth realm, that means the Earth and everything in it has to obey what God has said. When I say what God says I am speaking on behalf of God. 1st John 4:17 explains that because our love for God is perfected, we will have boldness in the day of judgement; and just as Jesus was on this earth, we will be just like him. God told Joshua to be bold, be courageous. So, I too will have boldness in the day of judgment so that as Jesus is in this world, so am I. Since I know what God word says about healing, I have no choice but to be bold I have no choice but to be confident, I have to say it and I must not be influenced by what I see, but only moved by what I believe, and what I believe is that God's word will not drop to the ground and be in vain. Regardless of whether it takes a day, a week, a month, or a year, I am telling you, God's word will come to pass!

One more example about speaking and believing .... I had another issue to use God's word on for another two years. I had a bone spur in my ankle. After the MRI, the doctor told me they could go in and perform surgery to shave the bone spur down. What was happening is that every time I hit it a certain way it was like a thousand knives were being stabbed into my leg. It was so bad at times that I would literally fall to the ground. The pain, and especially the falling, was so embarrassing. One day I was with my children. I stepped a certain way and hit the bone spur. My entire leg gave way and I fell right to the ground in pain. This happened periodically which is why I went to the doctor. So, he told me it could be taken care of by shaving it off but doing so would have me incapacitated possibly two or three months. After hearing the doctor tell me this, I just said thank you, thank you, thank you, and I left. I just left and did not schedule anything else, but I knew I needed to do something. So, I began to get God's word again concerning my healing and began to go through this same process again and I laid hands on my ankle like it says in Mark 16:18, and "you shall lay hands on the sick and they shall recover" and James, 5:14 said to "...anoint with oil and pray a prayer of faith...". So, I did that. I spoke the word of healing as in Psalms 107:20 to my ankle and I began to speak to my ankle. Remember Mark 11:23 says "...whosoever shall say to the mountain ...," well, this bone spur was my mountain. I spoke to my ankle every week; I spoke to my ankle every month for 2 years. I spoke to my ankle and during that time when I was speaking, I may have fallen two or three times but after that second year, I never had any problem with that ankle. It has been ten years now and, as a matter of fact, that ankle is stronger than the other ankle. I can still play basketball and at the time of this writing I am a 60-year-old man. I am telling you; you must believe and stand on Hebrews 10:23 and speak God's word, hold fast to God's word, and hold fast to your confession of faith. A confession of faith is a statement in agreement with God's word regardless of the circumstances or conditions of the situation. You must speak God's word because the angels hearken unto God's word. Your body will hearken unto God's word. The mountain will hearken unto God's word, but you must be consistent, you have to believe what the Word says and when you believe what the Lord says, I'm telling you, healing will manifest because, as He is, so are we in this world. So, my conclusion about healing and how to stay with it, continue with the Word and the Word will come to pass because God again is not a man that he should lie, or the son of man that he should repent, He said it, He'll do it. He spoke it, He'll bring it to pass.

WHAT DID GOD SAY ABOUT PROSPERITY?

First, He told me I was blessed in Christ in Abraham. Once I understood what he meant when he said I should hearken diligently to His word, which is His will and His word, I began to put that word in my heart and do like he told Joshua in Joshua 1:8, "This book of the law shall not depart out of thy mouth; but thou shalt meditate therein day and night, that thou mayest observe to do according to all that is written therein, for then thy shall make thy way prosperous, and then thou shalt have good success." Oh my God! I got excited all over again! I saw that He said I have the responsibility to make my way prosperous. I have the responsibility to have good success. It is not God's responsibility. God has already done what he said he would do. He has already done it! God does not live just in the now. God lives in an eternal now. God does not live in time. He lives in eternal time. He sees the end from the beginning. So, God had already blessed me. I found out in Ephesians 1:3 that he has blessed me with all spiritual blessings in heavenly places in Christ Jesus. Someone may ask, "Well what do you mean by spiritual blessings?" Is it about grace, or talking about the holy ghost, because that's about spiritual things? I say no. In the bible God told Jeremiah He knew him before he was in his mother's womb. So, in other words, John wrote in John 4:24 that God is a spirit and those that worship Him must do so in spirit and in truth. So, since God is a spirit and I come out of God, I must be spirit. In 1st Thessalonians 5:23 the apostle Paul said it this way, "...pray God sanctifies you wholly, spirit, soul, and body so that you become blameless to the coming of our lord". What this means is, when I came out of God, I was in spirit form first. He told Jeremiah before he even came out of his mother's womb, I knew him. How did God know him? By the spirit. He was in spirit form. So, when he said he blessed me, with all spiritual blessings, in heavenly places in Christ Jesus, that means as stated in Colossians 1:16 that God has created all things both visible and invisible. There are some things that I cannot see that God has already put out there, that belong to me, including my finances and money, among other things. I cannot see them in the natural, but for them to manifest in the spirit realm, I must agree with God. I must say what God's word says just as in 2Peter1:3, God has given me all things that pertain to life and godliness through the knowledge.

So now I have got to have the knowledge of what God said about my finances and my money. So, it brings me back to the book of the law that should not depart out of my mouth. I should take that word which is God's word and begin to say it daily and say what God's word said. See there is not only saying. In the book of James, it says do not just be a hearer of the word but be a doer of the word. Luke 6:38 says, "Give and it shall be given unto you, in good measure, pressed down, shaken together, and running over, so that men give unto your bosom...." So, there is a process and order that God has put into the earth realm. First Corinthians 14:40 says, "Let all things be done decently and in order." So, everything I do must line up with the order of God. That is why I had to be sure my motives were right and to be certain I understood what was said in James 1:17, that all good and perfect things come from the father above. God has already done everything that he will ever do, all I have got to do is work through the process, find out what he said about my money, what he says about my finances and begin to say what he said, believe what he said, act on what he said and what He said will come to pass. Galatians 6:7 tells us to not be deceived, God is not mock whatever man soweth, that shall he reap also. Galatians 6:9, reminds us to not to be weary when you do not see it happening like you want it to happen in the moment; Do not be weary in well doing; for in due season, you are going to reap if you do not faint first.

Therefore, we are not limited if we begin to understand how Jesus was not limited by the seasons. Jesus was the word manifested in the flesh. He was not limited by the season. There is no such thing as 'limitation' with the Creator. You produce when you are in the presence of the Creator, when you are in the presence of the word. We are not limited by season.

Now we must have the knowledge and understand what God has said about our finances; and, when you have this knowledge of what God has said, and you believe what God has said, and you confess what God has said, regardless of how you feel, regardless of what you have or don't have in your bank account, you begin to say what God's word has said and listen to what the scripture says again. It is a redundant, repetitive process.

Remember, Psalms 103:20 said the angels hearken to the voice of the word of God just like they hearken to make sure God's word doesn't drop to the ground. It is up to me to make sure God's word comes to pass concerning my healing, and to make sure God's word comes to pass concerning my prosperity because God told me in 3rd John verse two, "Beloved, I wish above all things that thou mayest prosper and be in health, even as thy soul prospereth." That's what God says to me, that he wishes (he prays) that above all things that I should prosper and be in good health, even as my soul prospers. He also said in Psalms 35:27, that God takes pleasure in the prosperity of his servant. I am a son that serves so God takes pleasure in me prospering, and therefore, he gave me the power to get wealth.

Once I began to learn the power of confessing God's word, and believing God's word, acting upon God's word, God's word cannot, and shall not return void. The Bible says in Ephesians the sixth chapter that having done all this "stand." Stand on what? Stand on what God has said. If we get off the foundation of God's word and what God has said, we will fail. When we begin to obey the scriptures and "Seek ye first the kingdom of God and his righteousness, ... all these things shall be added unto you." Matthew 6:33.

Here is another example of what happened when I began to confess God's word concerning my finances.

We were trying to purchase a home. Every time we were nearing the date to close on the house, the closing date would change, and it seemed as if we weren't going to be able to purchase our home. Also, during this time, while visiting Houston, Texas. we were attending a conference and during the Thursday night service they asked for an offering. Although we had already given an offering the two previous nights, Thursday night was Founders night. Everybody was giving their best offering. Some were giving a thousand dollars, and much more, of course, I did not have a thousand dollars but wanted to give another offering anyway. We decided we were going to give $300, although they were still asking for $1000. I did not have it, but something in my spirit told me to 'give a thousand.' Then I remembered the credit card. I had forgot I had been approved for a credit card with a credit limit of $2500. So, I decided I was going to give a thousand dollars on the credit card. I had never given or sown a thousand dollars before. I wrote the credit card numbers down and gave the $1000. We returned home from Houston on that Saturday and that Monday we received a phone call informing us we could close on the house and a date was set for February. At the closing, the lady we were buying the house from asked me if I would follow her to the bank. I followed her to the bank thinking she just needed me to be with her while she cashed her check. I really did not know what her intentions were, but I went in the bank and passed some idle time waiting for her to finish her business. After she came from the counter, she walked over to me and gave me a stack of money. "What is this? I asked her. She said, "This is yours. I am giving this to you." She walked out of the bank, she got in her car and left. I got in my car and went home. When I got home, I counted what she had handed me, and it was $38,000. Now keep in mind, she did not give any explanation or anything, she just gave me the $38,000 in cash. I had never held $38,000 in my hand in my life, and I was like, Oh My God! I showed my wife and then the spirit of God reminded me that I gave $1,000, the first time giving $1000. I gave that $1000 on my credit card and I did not feel too good about giving it, but I obeyed the Lord. Job 36:11 says "If 'I' obey and serve Him, 'I will' spend 'my' days in prosperity and 'my' years in pleasure." I am telling you that was a tremendous blessing. When I realized that this works, from that point on, I have been giving tithes and offerings whether I feel like giving or not giving. If it is a good cause, I give, because the principle as in Ecclesiastes the 11th chapter, tells us to cast your bread upon the water and in many days, it shall return. Galatians 6:9 says do not get weary in well doing; in due season, you're going to reap if you faint not. Luke 6:38, says give and it shall be given unto you. Deuteronomy 28:2 says all these blessings shall run you down and overtake you. I confess wealth and riches are in my house daily. I confess that the blessing of the Lord makes me rich and adds no sorrow with it. (Proverbs 10:22). I confess these words daily because that is what God said.

Remember what we said earlier, let God be true and every man be a liar even, if the man maybe you or may be me. We have got to let God be the truth in all things, confess what God's word says. There were times I was trusting him yet trembling in my flesh. Why? The Apostle Paul said in 1Corinthians 9:27 that I must put my body under subjection. I have got to obey God's word and do what it said. Because God's word is infallible. God's word will come to pass. God's word faileth not.

So, what did God say about my money? God said, "I wish above all things that you prosper and be in health even as your soul prosper." God says in Acts 20:35, "...it is more blessed to give than to receive." He tells us in Ecclesiastes that we should not wait until a good time to give but give at all times. Why? Because when we give, we should treat it as if we are giving to the Lord. The money may leave your hand, but it will never leave your life. In other words, when your heart is right towards God, and it is your desire to please him,

He'll bring you in the company of the people you need to know and into the acquisition of the knowledge that you need to have that is critical for your destiny and purpose in life. This was such a critical lesson for me; to find out what was God saying about my healing, and what God was saying about my money.

I needed to know what God was saying about my children. I have three children and eleven grandchildren, and I needed to find out what God said about my children because I did not want to be like Job; making sacrifices while operating in fear and being tormented dealing with things as a parent in this volatile world. I had to find out what God says about my children. I did not want to be up at night, walking the floor, out of worry. I did not need the panic and anxiety of what could be when I hear the phone ring, asking is it my son...is it my daughter...is it my other son...is it my grandchild? I did not need to be in that place of worry, in that place of stress, in that place of trepidation. I needed to be in a place of security. I needed to be in that place as described in Psalms 11:3 about having that solid foundation and God's word is more solid than anything else. Psalms 119:89 says, "Forever oh Lord is thy word settled in the heavens." I say forever oh God is thy word settled in me. So, I know that God's word is settled, and I'm settled in God's word...on God's words. John 15:7 says that if I abide in Him and His words abide in me, I can ask God for what I need, and it shall be done. I'll go back to David when he said in Psalm

119:105, "Thy word is a lamp unto my feet and a light unto my path;" and Psalms 19:14, "Let the words of my mouth and the meditation of my heart be acceptable in thy sight, oh Lord, my strength, and my redeemer."

Remember we said the same process to get the slice of bread, is the same process to get the loaf of bread. The same process to get the loaf, to get the slice and the factory is the same process to get the total business, in other words, to own the whole company. It is the same process. And remember what Jesus said, if you continue with this process, with my word, using the word associated with the subject matter you are dealing with, you shall be my disciple indeed. You shall own the company indeed. You shall own the company because it will make you free from the doubts, the fears, the stress, and anxiety.

So, I begin to use that same process to find out what God said about my children. Proverbs 22:6 said, "Train up the children in the way they should go and when they get old, they won't depart from the way." I found in Ephesian 6:1-3 where it says, "Children obey your parents in the Lord for this is right. Honor thy father and thy mother, for this is the first commandment with promise. That it may be well with thee, and thou mayest live long on the earth." I began to find this out in Isaiah 54:13 that "...my children should be taught of the Lord, and great shall be their peace..." Isaiah 54:17 says no weapon that is formed against my children will prosper and that every word that is spoken against them God will condemn. This is the heritage of the servants of the Lord, and their righteousness is of me, saith the Lord." I learned that I must confess what God said about my children. My children, our children are a godly heritage from the Lord. I had to confess what God said about my children and as I began to confess that and began to add to those confessions' verses such as Romans 5:5, which says "The love of God is being shared abroad in our heart (and my children's heart) by the Holy Ghost." I began to confess what the scripture said in 2Corinthians 4:4 the God of this world does not blind the heart of my children; that the glorious light of the gospel will shine unto them. I began to confess what God says about my children, that my children are being taught of the Lord and great shall be their peace. I begin to confess what God said about my children, that my children walk by faith not by sight. I begin to confess what God says about my children, greater is He that is in my children than he that is in the world. I begin to confess that which God says about my children and once you begin to confess and stand on what God's word says and stay with that process. Your children may have a lot of dumb days and they may make a lot of dumb decisions, but I found it to be true when I began to confess Psalms 115:14 --- he said, "The Lord shall increase you more and more, you and your children". In other words, when I begin to get increase and I confess that word daily, my children begin to increase also.

When I began to confess what God said and receive the knowledge of God, because when reading Hosea 4:6, it says that people are destroyed for a lack of knowledge. This is a critical lesson when talking to or about children. It is not that the knowledge is not available in this day and in this hour with all the many different platforms that we have available for learning. It is because we rejected God's knowledge and so God says that He rejects us from being a priest and from being an intermediary being...one that stands in the Gap or one that will make up the hedge. In other words, in this day and hour we can come boldly to the throne of grace, but, because we rejected the truth of God's word, we rejected the knowledge of God's word, we cannot come boldly. Then He said I reject 'you' and then also I will reject your children. And so, right now, I must make sure that I am not rejecting God's word, and I must speak God's word, and continue to stay in God's word with the knowledge of God's word.

WHAT DID GOD SAY ABOUT OUR CHILDREN?

Once I found out what God said about my children, when I am sitting around the table, when I'm walking down the street or whatever I'm doing, I must always be sharing the good things God has done. I must always share testimonies. Revelations 12:11 says, "They overcame him by the blood of the lamb and the word of their testimony." Many times, I must implement the knowledge of what God said, about how I am to root and to ground my children in the word of God. I remember 2nd Chronicles 20:20 says "...believe in the Lord your God and so shall you be established...". So, for my children to be established, for me to be established, I must believe, and I must exemplify that belief in front of my children and be an example for them. Remember, Matthew 5:14 says you are the light of the world. So, I am the light that my children will see.

What did God say about my children? He said I am to shine the light before them. Remember that light is revelation, light is knowledge, and you train them up in this knowledge. Once you begin to share with them the knowledge of what God says, I am telling you, they will begin to get roots. They will be like a tree planted by the rivers of water even though they may bend, they will not break. Why? Because you have followed the instructions of what God's word says about your children and I am telling you the scripture is true, it shall not return void, but it will accomplish and prosper the thing for unto where he sent it. The children, even though they may stray, you must begin to put the responsibility on the word of God and begin to cast out all your cares concerning your children on the Lord as 1st Peter 5:7 tells us. In other words, you are not being negligent, and you are not being complacent. You are being responsible; you are continually lifting up your children thanking God for what he has done for them; thanking God for the future things he will do; thanking

God that he's raising holy ghost witnesses to go across their path and witness to them and shine the glorious light of the gospel upon them. You are thanking God that he is protecting them from seen and unseen dangers. You are thanking God that they walk in victory, that they walk in faith, that they walk in the love of God; and that they thank God for those things. David said I will enter his gates with thanksgiving and into his courts with praise. So, you begin to specify and begin to say what God says concerning your children, just like you said what God said concerning your healing, and about your finances. What God says concerning your children, even when others have placed a low standard for your children and your children may be stereotyped in this world. I do not say what the world says about them. I only say what God said about them. That they are a godly heritage and that they shall be taught of the Lord. God said that my son will attend to his word. He will incline his ears to his sayings, he will keep the word of God before his eyes. He will hide the word of God in his heart. So, I'm going to do the affirmative.

One of the things that we must realize, as we stand on God's word, and confess God's word as we believe God's word, God will make sure Jeremiah 1:12 holds true that God said he hasten to perform his word. He will not allow his word to drop to the ground when we affirm his word by putting it in our mouth and saying exactly what he said, which is why it's so important to know what God says. We know what E.F. Hutton said, we know what Congress has said, we know what the legislators have said, we know what the governor says, we know what other actors, football players, NBA players, movie stars have said. But do we know what God said? God has the first word and the last word. So, when we know what God's word says and we stand on what God's word says, God will make sure his word comes to pass. It will accomplish the things where unto he sent it. And after learning that, I do not sit up at night. I do not worry. I do not bite my fingernails off because I cast out all my cares upon Him. I speak the word of God over my children and grandchildren. The angels are encamped around them. And when I pray for them, I don't pray desperation prayers. I just thank God and praise God that the work is already done; that he's fulfilling it. Just as I stood for a whole two years for that ankle bone spur, it came to pass. Just as I stood for a whole year for my healing from the cancer, it came to pass. Just as I stood on the promise of God concerning financial increase, it came to pass. All we must do is stick to what God says. Is it a fight? Is it a battle? Yes, it is. The apostle Paul said he had to fight the good fight of faith to finish his course. That is an example we must follow.

WHAT DID GOD SAY ABOUT LOVE?

So, what did God say about love? In this day and in this hour, we need the love of God like never before as it says in John 3:16. Because love is one of the things that will keep your heart right toward God. The Bible declared in Ecclesiastes the heart is evil and desperately wicked, who can know it? This is in reference about the heart of man and so I must realize that I have got to have the heart of God. The Bible declared that David was a man after God's own heart and this help me realize and better understand John 3:16, "For God so loved the world, that he gave his only begotten Son, that whosoever believeth in him should not perish, but have everlasting life." I know I am loved by God because 1st John 4:8 says God is love and I'm a child of God. John 1:12 tells me He gave me power to become a son of God. God made me and Genesis 1:26-28 lets me know that God made me in his very own image, in his very own likeness, and he gave me dominion over the fowl of the air, and the fish of the sea, and every creature that lives on the earth"; so I am made in the image of God. Therefore, I have the love of God. Reiterating 1st John 4:17 which says, "Herein is the love of God perfected; that I will have boldness on the day of judgement; that as he is, so am I in this world."

So that means I am love. I must operate and function in love. God says, I am love in the earth realm. I am a child of God. The bible says in 2nd Corinthians 5:17, "...if any man be in Christ, he is a new creature; old things are passed away; behold, all things are become new." Therefore, I am new. I have been made in love. I was made in sin when my mother and father came together, as far as the world is concerned, but when I gave my life to Christ, I was born again, and He made me love in the earth realm. So, when I follow the example of Jesus that means I am love, but I have got to acknowledge that. I have got to believe that I must exemplify that. So, in other words the Bible says I must pray for those that despitefully use me, and by doing this, others will know that I am His disciples, showing the love that I have for others.

What did God say about love? He said I am love in the earth realm. This is the love of God that brings us to maturity and Paul said it best... "When I was a child I spoke as a child, I acted like a child. I threw tantrums as a child but when I became a man, became mature, and became perfected to a certain degree, I began to operate in the love of God." Now we all know that the apostle Paul was once a serial killer by the name of Saul. He killed people from church to church before his conversion. But when he met the love of God on Damascus Road and he cried out, "Who art thou, Lord?" And God spoke to him and transformed his life and changed his name to Paul. And so the Apostle Paul, that same serial killer, became a new creature, old things had passed away. And guess what happened, he went back to some of those same churches and began to operate from love. Now he believed that God's love was greater than the evil he had done, because Paul stood up and said, I wrong no man. We read about him being a partaker in the death of Steven. Paul was operating in the love of God, Paul believed that God's love had forgiven him (Proverbs 10:12).

When Paul started preaching and keeping the gospel, lewd fellas came together by the way of Nazareth vowing to kill him. They bound themselves under a great curse and would not eat until they killed apostle Paul. On one occasion, to avoid the band of killers, Paul hid in a basket and was lowered down a wall to escape. On another occasion they stoned Paul and left him for dead. But Paul got up and continued in the love of God.

When Paul was on his way to Rome he was shipwrecked on the island of Malta. While on the ship a very violent storm arose and begin to toss the ship in every direction. The captain of the ship ordered that all the prisoners be killed so that none of them would escape if the ship was destroyed in the storm. Paul told the captain not to fear because an angel gave him instruction that if would stay on the ship no lives will be lost. The ship was destroyed, but everyone made it to safety.

Another story of God's hand on Paul was seen while he was warming himself around an open fire. A poisonous snake leaped out of the wood and bit him. Because this was a deadly snake everyone expected Paul to die. Paul shook the snake off into the fire and begin to share the love of God with the people of that Island.

There were so many things that happened to Paul, yet you could still see Paul operating in the love of God. So, we must operate in that same kind of love. We must truly operate in the kind of love Paul displayed, especially now in this present day when this world is full of hate, full of divisiveness, and full of all types of things that are happening in our world today.

What did God say about love? Love must be exemplified. We must walk in love. We must pray for those that despitefully use us; we must be love in the earth realm because only by this will men know that we are his disciples; that we love one another. One day some scholars asked Jesus what the greatest commandment was. Jesus told them that with all their heart, their soul, their mind, their might, and their strength they should love the Lord their God. He also told them that the second one is like the first one, that they must love their neighbor as they loved themselves. These two things stand true for us today, to love God and to love our neighbor as we love ourselves. I am to love everybody, every nationality, tall people, short people, even the wicked people of the world.

So, what did God say about love? I must be in love, I must walk in love, I must pray in love. I must give in love. I have even got to drive in love. I must always operate in love, even when I'm talking or when I'm writing. I must do it in love because, if it is not from a heart of love, it has the ability to become selfish and love should always be unconditional. Love is without expectation. The spirit of God shares this with me as I began to confess love, because I was like every other human being on the earth. Vengeance was mine and once I found out what God said, I had to deal with individuals that challenged that love. Individuals trying my faith time after time and there were times that I failed, but once I received and settled that word in me and confessed what God said about it, that settled the issue once I began to get it and understand. Psalm 119:89 says, "Forever oh Lord is thy word settled in the heavens." Therefore, I say forever oh lord is the word settled in me. It did not look good. It did not feel good. It made me look weak. It made me look as if I was a failure, but I already knew that in God there is no failure. God will always do what he said, it was already settled because he cannot lie. And so, once I began to handle the challenges of dealing with difficult people or situations by operating in love it often looked bad for me. In most of those situations, it looked like I was a weakling, but I guarantee you God always brought me to a place where I was able to have peace and sleep at night, I was able to continue to love those that despitefully used me; to pray for them. I will continue to do good unto people all because it is based on love. God said it had to be in love because God knows my heart, whether I am doing it to be seen, doing it to be heard, doing it for accolades, or when I am doing it from a pure heart, a heart of God. And when I do it from that standpoint, glory to God. When we operate in that kind of love it becomes a saving grace for humanity.

What did God say about love? He said the love of God has been shared abroad in my heart by the Holy Ghost. In other words, I speak in and with love, I live with and as love because God is love. We must remember what the scripture says in 1st John 4:17, "Herein is the love of God perfected; that in the day of judgement we may have boldness; that as he is, so are we in this world", and verse 18 says, "...perfected love cast out all fear...." What it does is cast out the fear of diseases. It will cast out the fear of the pandemic and of all the things that are happening in our world. Why? Because I am perfected in love. I am mature in what God said about love and I can only become mature in that if I believe what the word of God said about love and when I do that, it casts out all fear (which is "false evidence appearing real"). It casts fear out and I begin to rely on and trust in the Lord with all my heart. Matthew 13:19 says that when the word of God is sown and you do not understand it, then the wicked one will come and take that word, that is the knowledge of God's word. Then you do not have the knowledge. Psalm 119:105 says Thy word is a lamp unto my feet, and a light unto my path. And when you are not walking in the light, you're walking in darkness. And he that walketh in darkness stumbles. You see a lot of that is happening in our world today. So, what did God say about love? The love of God has been planted in our hearts by the Holy Ghost (Romans 5:5).

WHAT DID GOD SAY ABOUT THE KINGDOM?

When we investigate the scripture to find out what God says about the Kingdom, he says in Matthew 4:23 that Jesus went about in Galilee teaching and preaching in the synagogues the gospel of the kingdom and healing all manner of sickness and disease. In Matthew 4:17 while he was teaching his disciples, he went everywhere saying repent for the kingdom of heaven is at hand. There is another scripture that describes these days in which we live. In Matthew 24:3 the disciples asked Him what the signs of would be the coming of the kingdom, and of thy coming, and the end of the world. He responds in Matthew 24:14 with this answer, "And this Gospel of the kingdom shall be preached in all the world for a witness unto all nations; and then shall the end come." Now I want you to understand what God said about the kingdom. He said that the kingdom of God is at hand. He said that he came to bring his kingship, his rulership into the earth realm. When the disciples asked Jesus, in Matthew 6:9, to teach them how to pray, Jesus gave them a model prayer. He instructed them to pray, "...Our Father which art in heaven, hallowed be thy name. Thy kingdom come...." It was his desire that the kingdom of God be among men and that is what Jesus came to do...to set up the kingdom rule in the earth realm.

What did God say about the kingdom? He told the disciples to go into all the world and preach this Gospel of the kingdom. And when you begin to think about the kingdom, you think about God's rule, God's domain, God's authority. When you look at the kingdoms that are in this world right now, and you look at man's kingdom, and you look at some of the Lordships of Kings now, the Kings and prehistoric times, and even kings in this time, they took care of their citizens. They made sure that their citizens' needs were met. They conquered territory; they ruled and reigned and they had in place what we call a theocracy or monarchy whereby they controlled things. And so, Jesus said that we should preach the gospel of the kingdom and when we are talking about the gospel of the kingdom how does that apply to our life? I look back over my life and see that I heard what God was saying in the beginning, but I did not understand it at first. And when I began to dive in, dig deeper and study the word of God, I began to find out that God is always talking to us and trying to lead us, guide us, and give us knowledge. Whether we receive that knowledge or not, that knowledge is still available to us. At one particular time in my life, I began to receive that knowledge at the level of my comprehension. But when I began to receive openly and willingly, I began to receive the benefits of the knowledge of the kingdom. Now at this time I know there are different levels in the kingdom and Jesus said preach the gospel of the kingdom into all the world.

So, what does God say about the kingdom? He said it should be in the heart of man. In the Gospel of Luke, chapter 17:20-21, He said people will say, "Lo, there's the kingdom, or lo, here's the kingdom." But He is saying the kingdom of God comes not with observation, but the kingdom of God shall be in you." Now when we began to look at this scripture and examine it, I ask myself, "Is the kingdom of God in me?" To help with my answer, I went to Colossians 1:13 which states that God delivered me from the power of darkness and translated me into the kingdom of his dear Son. So, once I read that I have been translated into the kingdom of God, whether that is known to me or unknown to me, that is what God did in the spiritual sense. He transferred me, he translated me into the kingdom of his dear son. So, the kingdom is in me, and I am in the kingdom.

Well, what are some of the benefits of the kingdom? Well, when I become subject to kingdom law, kingdom dictates, kingdom commandments, kingdom rule, that is when I began to submit myself under God. Remember the Bible tells us in James 4:7, "Therefore submit yourself under God" and when you're submitting to the kingdom of God you're submitting to God, and when you're submitting to the word of God, you're submitting to the kingdom of God. So, submit yourself under God and you will be able to resist the rule, the reign, and the dictates of the ruler of this world. Once I began to do that, I became subject to the kingdom of God. And then while becoming a subject of the kingdom of God, I became what we call an officer in the kingdom of God. What do you mean by an officer? An officer is one that has what we call authority. In other words, I have been picked out, I have been pulled to the front of the line, I have been given credentials, I have been given citizenship. I am a citizen in the kingdom of God and because I am a citizen in the kingdom of God, God adopted me into his royal family. Look again at the scripture John 1;12. Do you remember what it says? It tells us to them that received Him, to them He gave the power to become the sons of God. So, what did God say about the kingdom? He said that when you get born again, you are delivered from the powers of darkness and translated into the kingdom of his dear Son. Whether you know it or do not know it, you are in the kingdom and the kingdom is in you. What did God say? He said you become a citizen of the kingdom; you become an officer in the kingdom, and then God says now you begin to operate under the authority of the kingdom. As I just mentioned John 1:12 said to them that receive Him to them he gave power to become a son of God; that word power means exousia which means authority; the authority to operate at the king's dictates. So, who am I in the kingdom of God? I am a child of God. I have been washed in the Blood of the Lamb and now as I began to follow the command of Jesus when he said to go into all the world and preach this Gospel of the kingdom and make disciples, that is what I did. I become a living testimony. I become a living epistle because I am a kingdom citizen.

But I want to digress for just a moment because there are many out there who are not a kingdom citizen, or what we call a subject of the kingdom, or kingdom officer. They are not operating in kingdom authority. In other words, they are kingdom outlaws. What do I mean when I say they are kingdom outlaws? This means anytime you disobey God's words, anytime you go against the rule and the reign of God, you become what we call outside of the parameters which God tells us he has laid the pattern out for us to operate in. Let us look at what it says in Job 36:11, "If you obey and serve Him..." and Isaiah 1:19, "If you're willing and obedient...", and 1 Corinthians 14:40 which says, "Let all things be done decently and in order." Order means God's systematic way of doing things. So, the kingdom has an order, the kingdom has a rule. This is what he told Joshua, he said this book of the kingdom shall not depart out of your mouth, but thou shalt meditate therein day and night; that you may observe to do according to all that is written there in and then you will make your way prosperous, and you will have good success. That success comes from the kingdom that God has delivered you into and because you are in the kingdom, you have every right to receive the benefits.

You have every right to the bonuses, the overflow, the increase, that the kingdom provides. Just like an earthly kingdom, the King watches over you. The King makes sure that your needs are met. That is what Jesus said in Psalms 23, where the Psalmist said, "The Lord is my shepherd I shall not want...". This scripture tells us that Jesus has already provided in his kingdom everything that we would ever need, want, or desire. It is found in the word let us look at a few scriptures, ... (Philippians 4:19). supply your every need...Psalm 23:1. I shall not want...Psalm 37:4 ...Delight yourself in the Lord. give you desires of your heart). Father means source, so the Father is the God of this kingdom.

Now what did God say about the kingdom? He said the kingdom of God is at hand. In reading Mark 1:14 it tells us, "Now after John was put in prison, Jesus came into Galilee preaching the gospel of the kingdom of God," and the kingdom of God is at hand. That is why Jesus went everywhere. So, this is what we're going to have to do. We are going to have to present the kingdom of God. There is only one real kingdom in this world. That is what Jesus delivered to us and that is what he told us to deliver to mankind. Why? Because in the kingdom of God there are not any needs or wants. Let us look again at the model prayer Jesus taught his disciples (Matthew 6:9-13), "Our Father which art in heaven hallowed would be thy name. Thy kingdom come; thy will be done in earth as it is in heaven. Give us this day our daily bread; ...Lead us not into temptation but deliver us from evil. For thine is the kingdom, and the power, and the glory, forever. Amen." It is the kingdom of God that sustains us. It is the kingdom of God that protects us. It is the kingdom of God that provides for us. It is the kingdom of God in which we draw our peace. It is the kingdom of God in which we get our prosperity because in the kingdom there is no want. There is no unease. There are no desires that will not be met. Why? Because God is the God of that kingdom. Jesus is Lord of that kingdom. That's why he said I'm Lord of Lords and I'm King of Kings. I am looking forward to the day when men, women, boys, and girls everywhere will begin to praise God in the kingdom of his dear Son and that kingdom will come and be on earth, even as it is in heaven, in a physical form. Now we look in the natural world and we don't see that kingdom setup. But when we begin to look by faith, we can see that the kingdom of God is at hand. If I stretch out my hand, I can see my hand. The kingdom of God is here, just like my hand is here. In Luke 17:21, Jesus has already warned us that people will say the kingdom is here or there. However, we have learned the kingdom of God will not be here or there, but in us. So, this is an old covenant in St. Luke, but now since I have been born again and have given my life to Christ, the kingdom of God is in me. I operate from that kingdom, that is living on the inside of me. I'm in the kingdom and the kingdom is in me and because of that, I can let my light shine. Because of that, I can begin to trust in the God of Abraham, Isaac, and Jacob. I can trust in God the Father and my Lord and Savior Jesus Christ, because I have a living reality that the kingdom of God has been made available unto me. The kingdom of God has been brought into my world because I accepted Jesus Christ as my personal Lord and Savior, and now, I am benefiting from that kingdom. And anybody at this time or a moment in life, can benefit from that kingdom, but you will never benefit from it until you know what God says.

What did God say about the kingdom? He said the kingdom of God is at hand. The gospel of the kingdom must be preached and hence the reason Isaiah 60:2 says darkness covers the earth and thick darkness is over the people. So now we must preach the kingdom, which is the kingdom of Life. Jesus said, "I am the light of the world; I am the way the truth and the light." In Matthew 5:16, He said we should let our light shine among men so that they may see our good works and glorify our Father in heaven. So, when we began to understand what God said about the kingdom, the kingdom must be lifted. The kingdom life must be shown in the earth realm. The kingdom of God is at hand and when we accept that call of the kingdom and know what God says about the kingdom, we will readily receive what God has made available to us, through the kingdom of God. That is healing for our body. It is prosperity for our ministries to help the needy and take care of the orphans and the widows. It is the peace God has given us amid confusion. He gives us joy during sorrow. He calls love to bubble from our hearts in the midst of a hate filled environment. All these things the kingdom provides. The kingdom has made everything that heaven represents available to the diaspora to us as men and women in this world. When we began to understand the kingdom of God and how it functions and operates in the earth realm, we will operate as Jesus operated in the earth realm.

So, what did God say it says? As God has spoken in sundry times and in divers' places, he's yet speaking to us now. He is saying spread the gospel of the kingdom. It is a kingdom mandate that we operate in kingdom authority, and we began to represent as kingdom citizens. We must become subject to the kingdom of God where we will begin to operate in the earth realm as a citizen of the most-high God, as being Ambassadors who represent our heavenly Father. The Bible declares that we are to imitate God as dear children. In Ephesians 5:1 it states, "Be ye followers of God as dear children." It also tells us in Hebrews 6:12, "...followers of them who through faith and patience inherit the promises." These are people that have tapped into the principles of the kingdom and are living out the promises of the kingdom; their inheritance is being manifested in their lives daily. God did not leave us comfortless. He left the kingdom of God to us so that we can live in this earth. Jesus prayed a prayer in John 17:17, "Sanctify them through thy truth, for thy word is truth." And verse 21 states, "Father I pray that they be one even as we are one...". Once we understand this, we become one with the Father and the kingdom by faith, that this is a faith walk, then we understand the kingdom of God is in us by faith. The working of the kingdom operates through us by faith. We submit to kingdom authority by faith. 1 John 5:4 says, "Whatsoever is born of God overcomes the world; and this is the victory that overcomes the world even our faith."

It is the faith from the kingdom of God; it is in the faith of God that we begin to operate and live a victorious life, healthy and prosperous. A life slated as a standard, that is put in a place for God, will be glorified. Where the word of God will be magnified, God can ask as he did of Job, "have you considered my servant...;" this is the day that God has made that we began to learn.

What did he say about the kingdom? He said the kingdom of God is at hand. On a final note, He says in the 24th chapter of Matthew "...this Gospel of the kingdom shall be preached into all the world for a witness unto all nations and then the end shall come." Matthew 24:12 says because iniquity does abound, the love of many shall wax cold. And for the many waxing cold, it is the kingdom that brings the light, the warmth, and the love of God into the darkness that is in our world and drives back the gross darkness that is upon the people. It is being in the kingdom of God that makes the difference. Without being in the kingdom many needs will not be met, without being in the kingdom many people will have sleepless nights because they don't know the joy of being under the covering, under the auspices, under what we call the 'soothing wings' of the kingdom of God that makes his people prosper in the midst of famine; that keeps his people healthy in the midst of a pandemic; that causes his people to rise to the top. And he knows that we suffered persecution, but because we are citizens of the kingdom, we can draw on its protection.

I am reminded of a story about the apostle Paul when he was being whipped; they were beating him, and Paul cried out and said, "Did you know that I'm a Roman citizen?" Back in that day, he paid a great price for Roman citizenship, and when he said, better yet, asked that question, the people dropped their whips. They began to treat Paul like he was somebody special all because he was a citizen of Rome. The devil has to back up once he understands that you know that you are a citizen of the kingdom of God, and you know that you have the authority that the kingdom authorized you with, and you are operating and subjected to the kingdom's mandate, you begin to recognize that you are an officer, and you can enforce the kingdom mandate in the earth realm, just like the apostle Paul. Paul said, "I'm a Roman citizen;" therefore, we can say daily, "I'm a citizen of the kingdom of God." And not only that, but I have been engrafted into the very family of the King. Jesus is my elder brother, and I am an heir of God and I'm a joint heir with Christ Jesus, all because God delivered me from the power of darkness and translated me into the kingdom of his dear Son. Now I am in the kingdom and the kingdom is in me and if I were to stand firm and be steadfast, unmovable abounding in the work of a kingdom, doing the work of the kingdom on a daily basis, that kingdom authority will began to rule and reign in my sphere of influence. Why? Because I give God access to use my hands, to use my feet, to use my voice, to use my abilities, my talents, my treasures, and to use my time to bring forth His will in the earth realm. And, because of that, I have been humbled, I have been blessed, I have been healed, I've been protected, all because I acknowledge this kingship. I acknowledge his kingdom. I just do not acknowledge it in a religious format, but I acknowledge it daily. I know the Bible says in Proverbs 3:5-6, "Trust in the Lord with all thine heart. Lean not to thine own understanding. In all thy ways acknowledge Him, and He shall direct your path." And once an individual begins to acknowledge the presence of God and acknowledges the kingdom of God, God begins to start a work in their lives. So now let us go back to the beginning.

IS GOD STILL SPEAKING TODAY?

God has spoken in divers' places and in sundry times, and God is still speaking today. Once we began to hear what he is saying, and begin to acknowledge what he is saying, believe what he said, act on what he says, what he says will come to pass, because God is not a man that he should lie, nor the son of man that he should repent. He hastens to perform his word and when my words come into agreement with his words, I take his words and replace my words with his words, that is when I began to agree with God. Take a moment to remember what Amos 3:3 asks... how can I walk with God if I am not in agreement with him, because how can two walk together except they be in agreement."

So, I began to make those confessions of faith and began to hold fast to what God has said, and what the kingdom of God has made available. I began to confess it repeatedly until it became a staple in my life. During this time as the kingdom of God became stable, steady, and unmovable in my life...all because of what God says.

There have been great statesmen, there have been great lecturers, there have been great orators that have spoken great words, exciting, and motivated thousands of people, but there is nothing that has moved me more than what God is saying, and has already said about my future, my health, my family, my finances, and my marriage. There is nothing more moving than what

God has said about the end times, what God has said about the Antichrist, even what God has said about presidential candidates. What God has said is all written in the Book. An author writing the memoirs of Jesus said that "if everything about Jesus Christ of Nazareth had been written in the Book, the world itself could not contain what He has said and what He has done."

So, God has spoken. God is yet speaking. All He's asking for us to do, to say, to believe is what Jesus said in Matthew 4:4, "It is written, man should not live by bread alone, but by every word that proceedeth out of the mouth of God." Let me show you how significant and powerful this is. In the beginning was the Word, and the Word was with God, and the Word was God, and now the Word became flesh and lived among men. Now here is that Word at the River Jordan being baptized by John the Baptist, and then here comes Satan trying to 'help' the Word. We must listen to the walking living Word, go to the written word, and speak the written word out into the atmosphere to combat and overthrow the forces of evil. Now that is powerful because the Word went to the word, and then spoke the word. So that's how important God's word is, and it should have a significant role in your life. In Matthew 6:33 Jesus reiterated that we should seek first the kingdom of God and its righteousness, and all these other things will be added to you.

Anyone who wants to get ahead in life, anyone who wants a successful career, successful marriage, successful business, it will be to their advantage to seek the kingdom of God, God's right way of doing things, and God's systematic way of doing things. God said because of his righteousness all these other things that you need, desire, and want, come to pass when you seek first the kingdom of God. And it all starts when we begin to find out what God says. No matter where you are, no matter what the subject is, when you find out what did God say and you learn what God is saying when he says in Revelation, "I have the first word and I have the last word, I am Alpha, and I am Omega, the beginning and the end." Once we conclude that God's word is forever settled in the heavens, then, God's word ought to be forever settled in us.

Psalms 138:2 sums it up. He said God has magnified His word above his name. And we know he is a wonderful counselor. We know he is a mighty God. We know he is an everlasting Father. We know that he is a Prince of Peace. We know that he is a Jehovah Rapha. We know that he is a Jehovah Shalom, Jehovah Tsidkenu, Jehovah Mekoddishkem Jehovah El Elyon, but He said I have magnified my word above my names. Please understand, the word of the Lord is a strong tower and when we, the righteous, run into it we are safe.

When we know what God says and begin to acknowledge what God says, begin to confess what God says, begin to believe what God says, and begin to act on what God says, God says that he will get in a hurry to perform his word to make sure that his words do not drop to the ground. So, when we understand that, "What did God say?" is not just a cliché but it is something that God has said in sundry times and divers' places, and he still speaks these words today. Let him that have ears to hear, hear what the spirit of God is saying. He is saying to the sinner, repent. He is saying to the sick, by the stripes of Jesus you are healed. He is saying to the saint, be strong in the Lord and in the power of his might. He is saying to the successful, give and it shall be given unto you. He is saying to the sincere, trust in the Lord with all your heart and lean not to your own understanding. He is saying to the doctor, I am a doctor. He is saying to the lawyer, I am your wisdom. God is still talking today. He is saying to those that are in trouble, I will show you a way that's better. I will lead you out of the dark into the marvelous light.

So, God is talking. The question is, are we hearing what God is saying? Someone is saying, well, what did God say about my marriage? What did God say about my business. What did God say about my children? What did God say about my health? What did God say about my ministry? What did God say about my career? What did God say about my wife? What did God say about the church I am a member of... God has said everything that needs to be said, and he has written all the answers in 66 books from Genesis to Revelation. And when we began to allow the word of Christ to become the meditation of our heart, and let it be in our mouth, and let it be a lamp unto our feet and a light unto our path, that word will lead us to the kingdom. The word will lead us to kingdom provisions. The word will lead us into kingdom protection. The word will lead us into kingdom prosperity. The word will lead us into kingdom peace. The word has already been loaded with everything that we need to be successful in this life.

What did God say? He is saying to us today, "look to Me." "Give your life to Me. Turn it over to Me and watch Me lift you out of the dung hole...lift you out of the darkness...lift you out of despair...lift you out of despondency...lift you out of the pains of death and bring you into the marvelous light where there is life forevermore."

What did God say in 1980, the second Sunday in October at 2:00 p.m. in the afternoon. This is when I gave my life to Christ and prior to this moment God was saying that I was lost and on my way to hell. He said that the wages of the sin that I was in was death. But He said the gift of God is eternal life. And when He said that to me, I believed Him. I believed Him in my heart. I confessed Jesus as Lord with my mouth, and He saved me. And since He saved me, he can save you. God takes you from where you are to where he wants you to be, but you must be willing to hear what he said, to hear what he is saying, and to hear what he said about your future. Today is the day of salvation. Harden not your heart. The day that you hear His voice that is the time. Do not put off for tomorrow what you can get done today, and if you are reading this book, and, if you're hearing this cry, God is speaking to you right now young man. God is speaking to you right now, young lady. God is speaking to you right now no matter where you are in the social status of life. God is speaking right now. Tone down the noise of confusion. Tone down the noise of division. Tone down the noise of all the clamor, all the clutter, all the corruption that is around you and begin to hear God saying, Come, unto me all ye who labor and are heavy laden and I will give you rest. He is calling out to you right now; what did he say? He said you do not have to stay where you are. What did he say? You can do better than what you are doing now. What did he say? He is saying the same thing that he has been saying throughout the years: if my people, which are called by my name, will humble themselves and pray, repent of their sins, turn from their wicked ways then I will hear you from heaven and I will heal your hurting body. I will heal your marriage. I will heal your business. I will heal your ministry. I will heal your land. That is what God is saying and he is still saying it. Jesus says, "I'm the same yesterday today and forevermore." He also says in Hebrews 13, "I'll never leave you nor forsake you." According to Mark 16:20, Jesus was always with the disciples. They went everywhere preaching the gospel and Jesus was with them confirming the word with signs. They believed what he said. And I am saying to you today, if you believe what God has said, and you take what God has said, confess it, and begin to apply it to your life, God will make sure that His word will be fulfilled in your life. That is a guarantee, not from me, it is a guarantee from what He said because God is a promise keeper. 2Corinthians 1:20 says, "All the promises of God are in Him, yes, and in Him Amen..." So, when you have the kind of confidence according to 1 John 5: 14-15, "This is the confidence that we have in him that if we pray according to his will, we know he hears us". And verse 15 tells us that since we know He hear us, we know we have the petitions that we have desired of him. It can be settled today that when you believe what God has said, because God's word cannot, shall not, will not return void, but it will accomplish that which I please, and it shall prosper in the thing whereto I sent it (Isaiah 55:11). When you know what God says, "just say what he said," and if you do not know what to say, just say what he said. If you do not know when to say it, just say what he said. And once you understand that and become one with that, watch God do some amazing things in your life. Watch God turn your business around. Watch God set your marriage straight. Watch God begin to move supernaturally in all areas of your life. That is a promise from the word of God for those that trust him, to those that rely on him. The scripture says-In Proverbs 16:3 "When you commit your works to the Lord, he will cause your plans to succeed."

I guarantee you when you began to find out what God says and began to act on what God says, God's word shall not and will not ever let you down. The scripture has already concluded that he has given to us all things that pertain to life and godliness, and all we must do is trust in Him. All we have got to do is lean upon him and put our total commitment, our total trust in him. The Bible says in Proverbs 16:25, "There's a way that seemeth right unto man, but the end thereof are the ways of death." When I began to do and say what God is saying through his Son Jesus. I began to follow his example. Jesus said that I am the way, I am the truth, I am the life. No man comes to the father except he comes by me. I am telling you when we begin to say what God says, when we begin to stand on what God says, when we begin to act on what God says, when we begin to believe what God says, his word shall come to pass, it shall manifest every promise that God has given us. I will reiterate that God is not a man that he should lie or the son of man that he should repent. He said it, He will do it. He spoke it, He will bring it to pass. God's word is true.

I am grateful and thankful that you have taken the time to read my book and allow God's word to become one in your life. When you ask yourself the serious questions about what God said about every issue in your life, you will be surprised that God has given you all the answers, but you must search them out. Remember in Matthew 5:6 Jesus said, "Blessed are they that hunger and thirst after righteousness for they shall be filled." And this is the TRUTH.

God bless you in your search to find out What Did God Say ABOUT YOU!

If you do not know Jesus Christ as your personal Lord and Savior, this is a good time to give your life to him. If I had not given my life to Jesus, I don't know where I would be today.

Ask him to come into your heart and forgive you of your sins. Do it now while you still have time. (Read Romans 10:9-13)

ABOUT THE AUTHOR

Alvin Deal is an author as well as senior pastor and founder of the Faith Christian Center Church in Greenwood, South Carolina. He is an anointed Man of God with more than 4o years of imparting biblical principles for daily application to life situations. His message is radical and compassionate that touches the unsaved, the unchurched, the uncommitted and the untaught. He is married to Georgia Deal where they press forward together in ministry. They have 3 children and 12 grandchildren.

www.ingramcontent.com/pod-product-compliance
Lightning Source LLC
Chambersburg PA
CBHW052117150726
48002CB00006B/2384